PRE-APPRENTICESHIP
MATHS & LITERACY FOR
GENERAL CONSTRUCTION

graduated exercises and practice exam

Andrew Spencer

A+ National

A+ National Pre-Apprenticeship Maths and Literacy for General Construction
1st Edition
Andrew Spencer

Publishing editor: Jana Raus
Project editor: Jana Raus
Proofreader: Tanya Simmons
Text designer: Miranda Costa
Cover designers: Lee Riches and Miranda Costa
Front cover image: iStockphoto/Goodluz
Back cover image: shutterstock.com/David Lee
Permissions researcher: Miriam Allen
Production controller: Adam Bextream
Reprint: Katie McCappin
Typeset by Q2A

Any URLs contained in this publication were checked for currency during the production process. Note, however, that the publisher cannot vouch for the ongoing currency of URLs.

For product information and technology assistance,
in Australia call **1300 790 853**;
in New Zealand call **0800 449 725**

For permission to use material from this text or product, please email
aust.permissions@cengage.com

ISBN 978 0 17 046450 5

Cengage Learning Australia
Level 7, 80 Dorcas Street
South Melbourne, Victoria Australia 3205

Cengage Learning New Zealand
Unit 4B Rosedale Office Park
331 Rosedale Road, Albany, North Shore 0632, NZ

For learning solutions, visit **cengage.com.au**

Printed in Australia by Ligare Pty Limited.
1 2 3 4 5 6 7 25 24 23 22 21

A+National
PRE-APPRENTICESHIP
Maths & Literacy for General Construction

Contents

LITERACY		

MATHEMATICS		

Introduction

It has always been important to understand, from a teacher's perspective, the nature of the mathematical skills students need for their future, rather than teaching them textbook mathematics. This has been a guiding principle behind the development of the content in this workbook. To teach maths that is *relevant* to students seeking accreditations and apprenticeships is the best that we can do, to give students an education in the field that they would like to work in.

The content in this resource is aimed at the level that is needed for students to have the best possibility of improving their maths and literacy skills specifically for trades. Students can use this workbook to prepare for an apprenticeship entry assessment, or to even assist with basic numeracy and literacy at the VET/TAFE level. Coupled with the activities on the NelsonNet website https://www.nelsonnet.com.au/free-resources, these resources have the potential to improve the students' understanding of basic maths concepts that can be applied to trades. These resources have been trialled, and they work.

Commonly used trade terms are introduced so that students have a basic understanding of terminology that they will encounter in the workplace environment. Students who can complete this workbook and reach an 80 per cent or higher outcome in all topics will have achieved the goal of this resource. These students will go on to complete work experience, do a VET accredited course, or be able to gain entry into VET/TAFE or an apprenticeship in the trade of their choice.

The content in this workbook is the first step to bridging the gap between what has been learnt in previous years, and what needs to be remembered and re-learnt for use in trades. Students will significantly benefit from the consolidation of the basic maths and literacy concepts.

Every school has students who want to work with their hands, and not all students want to go to university. The best students want to learn what they don't know; and if students want to learn, this book has the potential to give them a good start in life.

This resource has been specifically tailored to prepare students for sitting apprenticeship or VET/TAFE admission tests, and for giving students the basic skills they will need for a career in trade. In many ways, it is a win–win situation, with students enjoying and studying relevant maths for trades, and Registered Training Organisations (RTOs) receiving students who have improved basic maths and literacy skills.

All that is needed is patience, hard work, a positive attitude, the belief in yourself that you can do it and a desire to achieve. The rest is up to you.

About the author

Andrew Spencer has studied education both within Australia and overseas. He has a Bachelor of Education, as well as a Master of Science, in which he specialised in teacher education. Andrew has extensive experience in teaching secondary mathematics throughout New South Wales and South Australia for well over fifteen years. He has taught a range of subject areas, including Maths, English, Science, Classics, Physical Education and Technical Studies. His sense of the importance of practical mathematics continued to develop with the range of subject areas he taught in.

Acknowledgements

For Paula, Zach, Katelyn, Mum and Dad.

Many thanks to Mal Aubrey (GTA) and all training organisations for their input.

To the De La Salle Brothers for their selfless work with all students.

Thanks also to Dr Pauline Carter for her unwavering support for all Maths teachers.

This is for all students who value learning, who are willing to work hard and who have character … and are characters!

LITERACY

Unit 1: Spelling

Short-answer questions

Specific instructions to students

- This is an exercise to help you identify and correct spelling errors.
- Read the activity below and then answer accordingly.

Read the following passage and identify and correct the spelling errors.

The forklift is an unbalenced mechine that has one end havier than the other end. The forklift should never be alowed to have more waight foreward of the centre of the front aksle than behind it. If the center of gravity of the forklift and the load combined moves forward what is known as the fulkrum, the forklift is in danger of tiping forward. Turning with the tines at height and on full back tilt may also cause a forklift to tip over.

Some causes of forward instabality may also include the folowing: overloading the forklift with too much weight; placing a rated load too far forwerd or unevenly on the tines; rough or inapropriate use of hoist and tilt levers; lifting with forward tilt on the mast; violemt or uneven stopping and starting; operating the forklift on poor or uneven ground surface; and driving on an incline.

As with forward stabillity, the centre of gravity of the machine needs to be considered at all times when operating a forklift. Should the centre of grevity of the machine shift too far to one side or the other, the forklift may tip to one side.

Sideways instability may also ocur and be caused by: the load of the forklift is not centralised or in the middle of the tines; driving or working across an inclyne; carrying a load that is considered too high; turning on an incline; turning at unresonable speed for the forklift; uneven tyre pressures in one or more of the tyres; and opereting the forklift on a poor ground surface.

Incorrect words:

Correct words:

Unit 2: Alphabetising

Specific instructions to students

- In this unit, you will be able to practise your alphabetising skills.
- Read the activity below and then answer accordingly.

Put the following words into alphabetical order.

White card	Hazardous goods
Crane	Green card
Earthmoving	Bricklaying
Manual handling	Concreting
Scaffold	Lifting equipment
Restraint	Confined spaces
Height safety	Blocklaying

Answer:

_____

_____

_____

_____

_____

_____

_____

_____

_____

_____

_____

_____

_____

_____

Shutterstock.com / Cynthia Farmer

Unit 3: Comprehension

Read the following passage and answer the questions in full sentences.

'Big Kev', as he is known by his fellow workers due to his 'big heart', is the site manager on a major construction worksite. He is in charge of overseeing the building of an apartment block in the middle of a bustling city. He has a dedicated, experienced crew working under him who is always punctual and reliable. Stratos, Rocco, Den, Chris and Li'l Eddy are the construction workers on the morning shift that begins at 7 a.m. each day and Tony is their supervisor.

Big Kev knew Friday was going to be a busy day as he had several trucks coming onto the site to deliver steel beams, and he needed his crew to unload the beams so that the welders could get them into place and weld them. Like clockwork, the trucks arrived on time and Tony, the 'Old Choc' as he was known by his fellow workers, operated the crane as he unloaded the beams at a steady rate. Stratos and Rocco got in the boom lift and put on their fall arrest harnesses and then went up to secure the first beam before welding it.

Meanwhile, Den and Chris began painting those beams that had already been welded in place on the previous day. Li'l Eddy climbed into the driver's seat of the forklift and began cleaning up the debris left from the previous day. By the morning break at 9.45 a.m., everyone on the crew had completed a lot of work and they were keen to sit and have a well-earned break. After the break, Tony wanted scaffolding erected to allow for some electrical work to be completed before lunch.

The crew all knew that the weather was starting to get worse and that they needed to get as much done as possible before the rain began. Just as the break was coming to a close, it began to rain heavily. The site became inundated with water and soon it was unsafe to continue with construction. The crew would need to return early the next day to catch up on the work that had been halted due to the weather.

QUESTION 1

Who is Big Kev and what is his role on-site?

Answer:

_____

QUESTION 2

At what time does work begin each day and who is the supervisor?

Answer:

_____

QUESTION 3

On this day, what job did each member of the crew have on-site?

Answer:

_____

_____

QUESTION 4

How long had the crew worked for before they had their morning break?

Answer:

_____

_____

QUESTION 5

Why did work stop for the day on the worksite?

Answer:

_____

MATHEMATICS

Unit 4: General Mathematics

Short-answer questions

Specific instructions to students

- This unit will help you to improve your general mathematical skills.
- Read the following questions and answer all of them in the spaces provided.
- You may not use a calculator.
- You need to show all working.

QUESTION 1

State the unit of measurement that you would use to measure:

a   the length of a steel rod

Answer:

_____

b   the temperature of a truck engine

Answer:

_____

c   an amount of oil

Answer:

_____

d   the weight of a load

Answer:

_____

e   the voltage of a battery

Answer:

_____

f   the length of an extension cord

Answer:

_____

g   the volume of concrete.

Answer:

_____

Alamy / © Mike Stone

QUESTION 2

Give examples of how the following might be used in the construction industry.

a   percentage

Answer:

_____

b   decimal

Answer:

_____

c   fraction

Answer:

_____

d mixed number

Answer:

_____

e ratio

Answer:

_____

f angle

Answer:

_____

QUESTION 3
Convert the following units.

a 12 kg to grams

Answer:

_____

b 4 tonnes to kilograms

Answer:

_____

c 120 cm to metres

Answer:

_____

d 1140 mL to litres

Answer:

_____

e 1650 g to kilograms

Answer:

_____

f 1880 kg to tonnes

Answer:

_____

g 13 m to centimetres

Answer:

_____

h 4.5 L to millilitres

Answer:

_____

QUESTION 4
Write the following in descending order.

0.4   0.04   4.1   40.0   400.00   4.0

Answer:

_____

QUESTION 5
Write the decimal number that is between:

a 0.2 and 0.4

Answer:

_____

b 1.8 and 1.9

Answer:

_____

c 12.4 and 12.6

Answer:

_____

d 28.3 and 28.4

Answer:

_____

e 101.5 and 101.7

Answer:

_____

QUESTION 6
Round off the following numbers to two (2) decimal places.

a 12.346

Answer:

_____

b 2.251

Answer:

_____

c 123.897

Answer:

_____

d 688.882

Answer:

_____

e 1209.741

Answer:

_____

QUESTION 7
Estimate the following by approximation.

a $1288 \times 19 =$

Answer:

_____

b $201 \times 20 =$

Answer:

_____

c $497 \times 12.2 =$

Answer:

_____

d $1008 \times 10.3 =$

Answer:

_____

e $399 \times 22 =$

Answer:

_____

f $201 - 19 =$

Answer:

_____

g $502 - 61 =$

Answer:

_____

h $1003 - 49 =$

Answer:

_____

i $10\,001 - 199 =$

Answer:

_____

j $99.99 - 39.8 =$

_____

QUESTION 8
What do the following add up to?

a $4, $4.99 and $144.95

Answer:

_____

b 8.75, 6.9 and 12.55

Answer:

_____

c 65 mL, 18 mL and 209 mL

Answer:

_____

d 21.3 g, 119 g and 884.65 g

Answer:

_____

QUESTION 9
Subtract the following.

a 2338 from 7117

Answer:

_____

b 1786 from 3112

Answer:

_____

c 5979 from 8014

Answer:

_____

d 11 989 from 26 221

Answer:

_____

e 108 767 from 231 111

Answer:

_____

QUESTION 10
Use division to solve the following.

a 2177 divided by 7

Answer:

_____

b 4484 divided by 4

Answer:

_____

c 63.9 ÷ 0.3

Answer:

_____

d 121.63 ÷ 1.2

Answer:

_____

e 466.88 ÷ 0.8

Answer:

_____

The following information is provided for question 11.

To solve using BODMAS, in order from left to right, solve the Brackets first, then Of, then Division, then Multiplication, then Addition and lastly Subtraction. The following example has been done for your reference.

Shutterstock.com/Jim Parkin

QUESTION 11

Using BODMAS, solve the following.

a $(6 \times 9) \times 5 + 7 - 2$

Answer:

_____

b $(9 \times 8) \times 4 + 6 - 1$

Answer:

_____

c $3 \times (5 \times 7) + 11 - 8$

Answer:

_____

d $5 \times (8 \times 3) + 9 - 6$

Answer:

_____

e $7 + 6 \times 3 + (9 \times 6) - 9$

Answer:

_____

f $6 + 9 \times 4 + (6 \times 7) - 21$

Answer:

_____

Unit 5: Basic Operations

Section A: Addition

Short-answer questions

Specific instructions to students

- This section will help you to improve your addition skills for basic operations.
- Read the questions below and answer all of them in the spaces provided.
- You may not use a calculator.
- You need to show all working.

QUESTION 1

A bricklayer bought a brickie's brush for $20, 3 sets of gloves for $38 and a brick carrier for $28. What would the total be?

Answer:

QUESTION 2

Bricklayers buy the following at a sale: 2 profile arm sets for $60, an axis door gauge for $18, 3 turbo 230 mm diamond blades for $120 and a brick trowel for $50. What is the total?

Answer:

QUESTION 3

A supply manager stocks 127 fluoro shirts, 268 pairs of safety glasses and 323 various pairs of disposable gloves. How many items are in stock in total?

Answer:

QUESTION 4

An order picker completes 35 orders in the first hour, 45 orders in the second hour, 15 orders in the third hour, 17 orders in the fourth hour and 45 orders in the fifth hour. How many orders have been filled in total?

Answer:

QUESTION 5

A forklift driver takes the following amount of time to complete the shifting of different-sized loads in a warehouse: load 1 in 35 minutes, load 2 in 45 minutes, load 3 in 75 minutes and load 4 in 30 minutes. How much time has been taken? (Give your answer first in minutes, and then in hours and minutes.)

Answer:

QUESTION 6

A worker loads materials onto four different trucks. It takes the following amounts of time to complete each load: truck 1 – 25 minutes, truck 2 – 35 minutes, truck 3 – 45 minutes, and truck 4 – 25 minutes. How much time has been spent by the worker loading materials onto the four trucks? (Give your answer first in minutes, and then in hours and minutes.)

Answer:

QUESTION 7

A person wants to get a statement of attainment for using the boom-type elevated work platform. She takes the following time to study certain units: handout on hazard management – 35 minutes; introductory notes – 15 minutes; instructions on setting up and operating EWP – 49 minutes; shut-down and clean-up procedures – 15 minutes; outline of emergency procedures – 45 minutes; and planning and preparing work for EWP operation – 79 minutes. What is the total time taken for reading?

Answer:

QUESTION 8

A building company buys a 1 kg fire extinguisher for $33 and a fall arrest harness for $206. How much is charged to the company's account in total?

Shutterstock.com / ChristineGonsalves

Answer:

_____

QUESTION 9

Two workers require 10 disposable polypropylene coveralls that cost $3 each, and a pair of safety boots each that cost $60 a pair. What is the total for both workers?

Answer:

_____

QUESTION 10

A full-face respirator is purchased for $289, a cooling vest for $205 and microfibre polo shirt for $19. How much does the total come to?

Answer:

_____

Section B: Subtraction

Short-answer questions

Specific instructions to students

- This section will help you to improve your subtraction skills for basic operations.
- Read the following questions and answer all of them in the spaces provided.
- You may not use a calculator.
- You need to show all working.

QUESTION 1

A concrete company purchases three 500 mm concrete rake spreaders for $128. How much change is given from $150?

Answer:

_____

QUESTION 2

Two 900 mm bull floats are bought for a total of $135. How much change is given from $200?

Answer:

_____

QUESTION 3

A bricklayer purchases a near new 14 inch brick saw with a 1700 W electric motor with stand, and mitre guide for a total cost of $1255. How much change would you get from $1500?

Answer:

_____

QUESTION 4

A worker uses twenty-seven 10 mm dyna bolts from a box that contains 150 dyna bolts. How many are left?

Answer:

_____

QUESTION 5

A company purchases 12 broad heel trowels for $425. The manager of the trade store takes off a discount of $35.00. How much does the customer need to pay?

Answer:

QUESTION 6

An apprentice uses 31 coach bolts on a commercial building project from a box that contains 50 coach bolts. How many are left in the box?

Answer:

QUESTION 7

A welder uses the following welding rods on-site on different jobs: 5, 3 and 6. How many rods are left from a packet that had 15 rods in it to begin with?

Answer:

QUESTION 8

Workers on a construction site use 74 pairs of gloves over three months. The box initially contained 93 pairs of gloves. How many are now left?

Answer:

QUESTION 9

The overall yearly budget for personal protective equipment (PPE) gear for a major crew of workers is $132 432. The actual cost of PPE gear came to $78 968. How much was left in the budget?

iStockphoto / fcafotodigital

Answer:

QUESTION 10

A bag contains 1400 nails. If 110 are used over two months, how many remain in the bag?

Answer:

Section C: Multiplication

Short-answer questions

Specific instructions to students

- This section will help you to improve your multiplication skills for basic operations.
- Read the following questions and answer all of them in the spaces provided.
- You may not use a calculator.
- You need to show all working.

QUESTION 1

If two 20 mm dyna bolts were used on one section of a building, how many would be used on 25 sections of the same building?

Answer:

QUESTION 2

If a 12 mm dyna bolt costs $0.55, how much would 50 cost?

Answer:

9780170464505

QUESTION 3

A 65 mm × 600 mm wood float costs $17 each. What will be the total cost for five floats?

Answer:

QUESTION 4

Six 115 mm brick bolsters were purchased for $15 each. What was the total cost?

Answer:

QUESTION 5

A construction worker is paid $29 per hour. What would be his total pay if he worked 13 hours at this rate over two days during the week?

Answer:

QUESTION 6

A shift supervisor buys seven brick hammers with hickory handles at a cost of $45 each. What will be the total cost?

Answer:

QUESTION 7

Construction site workers use nine tubes of silicon, on average, each day while working on-site. How many tubes would be used over a 31-day month?

Answer:

QUESTION 8

A fencing contractor used twenty-seven 20 kg bags of rapid-set cement each week. How many would be used over a 28-day month?

Answer:

QUESTION 9

A painting contractor used three bottles of thinners each week, on average. How many bottles would he use over a year? (Hint: There are 52 weeks in a year.)

Alamy/© Art Directors & TRIP

Answer:

QUESTION 10

A supervisor purchases seven elastic chin straps for his worker's safety caps. If each one costs $2, how much will all seven cost?

Answer:

Section D: Division

QUESTION 1

Twenty-four workers are booked in for a WHS (Work Health and Safety) seminar. If there are four rooms for the seminar, how many workers will be in each room?

Answer:

QUESTION 2

If an apprentice earned $568 (before tax) for a six-day working week, how much would he earn per day?

Answer:

QUESTION 3

A site manager purchases sixty 1 L bottles of sunscreen. If each box contains 12 bottles, how many boxes are there?

Answer:

QUESTION 4

A worker uses 720 coach bolts over three months. How many bolts is that, on average, per month?

Answer:

QUESTION 5

A bricklayer uses 180 red bricks to finish off 10 walls. How many bricks is that per wall?

Answer:

QUESTION 6

If one month's takings for Bert the Brickie's business was $15 677, how much were the takings, on average, per week? (For this question you can assume that there are four weeks in each month.)

Answer:

QUESTION 7

At a yearly stocktake, a storeperson at a warehouse counts 78 wool bound disposable dust goggles. If they were packed so that there were six in each box, how many boxes would there be?

Answer:

QUESTION 8

Thirty-six 12-piece drill sets are ordered in for a company. If there are six supervisors, how many sets will each supervisor get?

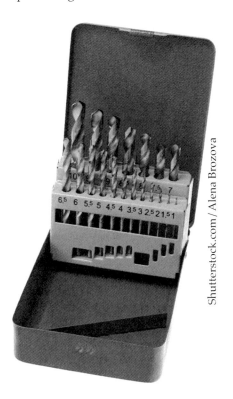

Shutterstock.com / Alena Brozova

Answer:

QUESTION 9

If a hire company hires out an 8 tonne 20 foot tray with crane and the bill comes to $1770 for 6 days, how much will the hire rate be per day, on average?

Answer:

QUESTION 10

A construction company uses 156 Unisafe terry towelling sweat bands for safety caps over a year. How many sweat bands is that per month?

Answer:

Section A: Addition

QUESTION 1

If four grooved plugging chisels are purchased for $75.20 and six cold chisels are purchased for $59.70, what is the total for the purchases?

Shutterstock.com/Miroslav Hlavko

Answer:

_____

QUESTION 2

A bricklayer purchases two brickie's brushes with end scrapers for $22.95, a 230 mm diamond blade for $18.95, a 99 L brickie's barrow for $294.55 and a large dust removal blow-out pump for $69.50. How much has been spent in total?

Answer:

_____

QUESTION 3

A site manager purchases a 1200 mm level for $102.50 and a 600 mm heavy-duty level for $53.75. What is the total cost?

Shutterstock.com/Laborant

Answer:

_____

QUESTION 4

Chemical splash goggles cost $5.95 each and a square mouth, long fibreglass handle shovel costs $48.50. What is the total cost?

Answer:

_____

QUESTION 5

A handyman buys the following: a 100 × 3.0 × 15 mm cut-off disk for $1.99, a string line no. 8 × 100 mm for $5.50, three 300 mm profile clamps for $46.50 and a 230 mm × 75 mm slimline vent for $3.95. What is the total cost?

Answer:

_____

QUESTION 6

The following items are on special and a customer decides to buy one of each: a pair of size-10 blue gloves for $5.95, a jointer 10 mm flat for $10.75 and a 200 × 80 mm F clamp for $9.50. How much do the purchases total?

Answer:

_____

QUESTION 7

A manager purchases the following items: a brickie's dummy clamp 300 m external for $14.50, an elastic chin strap for a safety cap for $2.95, four 105 × 1.0 × 16 mm cut-off disks for $5.95 and inject mortar for $13.75. What is the total cost?

Answer:

_____

QUESTION 8

A welder needs to cut three different lengths of steel rod. The rods need to be shortened by 10.75 mm, 7.85 mm and 8.50 mm, which will become wastage. How much steel rod will become wastage in total?

Answer:

_____

QUESTION 9

A paint store sells the following to a painter: a packet of steel wool costing $7.85, three extreme oval cutters for $31.65, a sash cutter for $10.45, six 120 mm special effects brushes for $59.95 and a winged scrubbing brush for $5.75. What are the total sales?

Answer:

_____

QUESTION 10

A gyprock shop's daily takings over a six-day week are $889.90, $945.50, $1555.50, $2135.50, $732.50 and $569.25. What are the total takings at this shop for the week?

Shutterstock.com / Jerry Portelli

Answer:

_____

Section B: Subtraction

Short-answer questions

Specific instructions to students

- This section will help you to improve your subtraction skills when working with decimals.
- Read the following questions and answer all of them in the spaces provided.
- You may not use a calculator.
- You need to show all working.

QUESTION 1

A customer purchased $38.65 worth of decorating supplies at a paint supplies shop. What change would be given from a $50 note?

Answer:

_____

QUESTION 2

An apprentice painter gets paid $568.50 for a week's work. Of this, $78.50 is used to pay the bills, $45.75 is paid for petrol and $126 is used on entertainment. How much money is left?

Answer:

_____

QUESTION 3

A customer purchases two corrugated wire brushes with handles for $63.50. The customer pays with a $50 and a $20 note. How much change is given?

Answer:

_____

QUESTION 4

An apprentice painter works 38 hours and earns $445.60. Of this, $34.75 is used for petrol and $84.50 for entertainment. How much is left?

Answer:

_____

QUESTION 5

Three painters walk into a trades store together and purchase the following items: four heavy-duty extension poles for $65.50, five paint plate roller ramps for $53.50 and two floor applicator replacement pads for $27.95.

a   What is the total?

Answer:

_____

b   One painter pays for all three items with three $50 notes. How much change is given?

Answer:

_____

QUESTION 6

Two 180 mm decking roller kits are purchased for $22.50. The customer pays with two $20 notes. How much change is given?

Answer:

_____

QUESTION 7

A worker needs four dripless industrial-type caulking guns to finish off some renovations on a friend's house. The guns cost $125.50 in total. What change is given if two $100.00 notes are used to pay the bill?

Answer:

_____

QUESTION 8

A renovator purchases a decking kit for a large outside area for $315.50 and a single pack of rubberised non-slip coating for $40.80. Exterior varnish stain is also bought for $30.25. The items are paid for from the renovator's budget, which has $518.55 in it before the purchases. How much remains in the budget after the purchases are paid for?

Answer:

_____

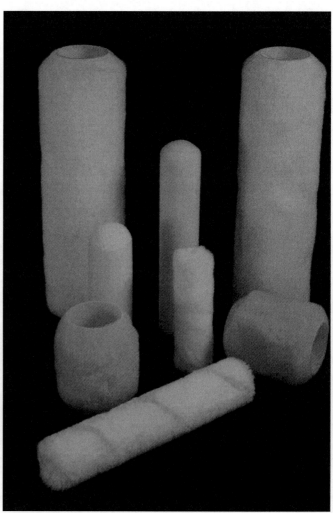

QUESTION 9

A paint roller frame is purchased for $36.50, pre-treatment primer for $29.50 and a twin pack of 110 mm fabric cover for $9.50. If four $20 notes are used to pay the bill, how much change is given?

Answer:

QUESTION 10

A professional aluminium pole sander costs $24.50, a diamond float costs $12.75, a smooth coat brush costs $5.95 and a 160 mm gloss roller kit costs $11.75. If the customer pays for these items with two $50 notes, how much change is given?

Answer:

Section C: Multiplication

Short-answer questions

Specific instructions to students

- This section will help you to improve your multiplication skills when working with decimals.
- Read the following questions and answer all of them in the spaces provided.
- You may not use a calculator.
- You need to show all working.

QUESTION 1

If one 105 surface filler costs $15.95, how much will five cost?

Answer:

QUESTION 2

A handyman purchases a 12 pack of 12 mm foam sanding pads, costing $9.50 each. How much will six packs cost?

Answer:

QUESTION 3

A tiler purchases six packs of tack cloth at a cost of $1.95 each. What is the total cost?

Answer:

QUESTION 4

A painting supervisor purchases eight 4 L tins of exterior low-sheen white that cost $69.95 each. What is the total cost?

Answer:

QUESTION 5

A customer buys two accessories starter kits from a paint supply store valued at $249.95 each. What is the total cost?

Answer:

QUESTION 6

Six people purchase a 4 L tin of wash-and-wear low sheen that is on special for $35.50. What is the total cost?

Answer:

QUESTION 7

A traffic control contractor buys 13 containers of road-marking paint that costs $67.50 each. What is the total cost?

Answer:

QUESTION 8

One pack of several different types of abrasives costs $30.95. How much will five packets cost?

Shutterstock.com / Brian Eichhorn

Answer:

_____

organisation and the cost is $125.75 each. How much will the total bill be for the group?

Answer:

_____

QUESTION 9

A group of seven Year 12 vocational education training students are paying for their two-day WHS in-service. They all book in with their registered training

QUESTION 10

Four 380 mL applicator guns are purchased for completing work on-site for $32.50 each. What is the total bill for the four applicator guns?

Answer:

_____

Section D: Division

Short-answer questions

Specific instructions to students

- This section will help you to improve your division skills when working with decimals.
- Read the following questions and answer all of them in the spaces provided.
- You may not use a calculator.
- You need to show all working.

QUESTION 1

A demolition team works on a house for six days and bills the owners $3628.55. How much is the daily average charge for the six days?

Answer:

_____

QUESTION 2

An apprentice gyprocker earns $590.60 for a five-day week. How much does he earn per day?

Answer:

_____

QUESTION 3

A tiler quotes $5785.50 for labor and materials for tiling a bathroom that will take five days to complete. How much does this work out to per day?

Answer:

_____

QUESTION 4

Three vocational education students attend a seminar on safety, focusing on how to wear PPE gear correctly on-site. If the people who run the course charge a total of $165.90, how much does each student need to pay if they are charged the same amount?

Answer:

_____

QUESTION 5

Three 230 mm turbo diamond blades are purchased by a contractor at a total cost of $90.90. How much does each blade cost?

Answer:

_____

9780170464505

QUESTION 6

A paving company buys four clamped handle screeds with 1.2 m level vial costing $336.80. How much does each cost?

Answer:

QUESTION 7

Six 36 inch power trowel blades are bought for a wacker machine. The total comes to $393.60. What is the cost of each blade?

Answer:

QUESTION 8

A construction manager purchases five 300 × 27 mm cold chisels at a hardware store. The total charged by the store is $93.75 for all five. How much is the individual price of each chisel?

Shutterstock.com/Ugorenkov Aleksandr

Answer:

QUESTION 9

Eight jointers 8 mm flat with soft fell handles and finger guards are purchased by a bricklayer for his crew for a total of $96.80. How much is the cost of each jointer?

Answer:

QUESTION 10

Three arm sets with sliding arm are needed on a building worksite. They are purchased for a total of $86.85. How much is each set?

Answer:

Unit 7: Fractions

Section A: Addition

Short-answer questions

Specific instructions to students

- This section is designed to help you improve your addition skills when working with fractions.
- Read the following questions and answer all of them in the spaces provided.
- You may not use a calculator.
- You need to show all working.

QUESTION 1

Solve $\frac{1}{2} + \frac{4}{5}$.

Answer:

_____

QUESTION 2

Solve $2\frac{2}{4} + 1\frac{2}{3}$.

Answer:

_____

QUESTION 3

A gyprocker uses $\frac{1}{4}$ tube of silicone on one bathroom wall and $\frac{1}{3}$ of a tube of the same silicone on the other wall. What is the total amount used on both walls?

Answer:

_____

QUESTION 4

Two bottles of thinners are each $\frac{1}{3}$ full. How much is there in total?

Answer:

_____

QUESTION 5

A paint tin of low-sheen white has $\frac{2}{3}$ left in it after completing a bedroom. Another tin of the same paint has $\frac{1}{4}$ left in it and is added to the first tin. How much paint is there in this first tin in total?

Answer:

_____

Section B: Subtraction

Short-answer questions

Specific instructions to students

- This section is designed to help you improve your subtraction skills when working with fractions.
- Read the following questions and answer all of them in the spaces provided.
- You may not use a calculator.
- You need to show all working.

QUESTION 1

Solve $\frac{2}{3} - \frac{1}{4}$.

Answer:

QUESTION 2

Solve $2\frac{2}{3} - 1\frac{1}{4}$.

Answer:

 9780170464505

QUESTION 3

A 20 L container of diesel fuel is $\frac{2}{3}$ full. If $\frac{1}{3}$ is used, how much diesel fuel is left in the container?

Answer:

_____

QUESTION 4

A painter has $2\frac{1}{2}$ containers of decking oil. If $1\frac{1}{3}$ is used on two different decks, how much of the decking oil is left?

Shutterstock.com/Paul Yates

Answer:

_____

QUESTION 5

A demolition company has $2\frac{3}{4}$ bottles of methylated spirits for use on-site. If $1\frac{1}{2}$ bottles are used, how much of the methylated spirits is left in total?

Answer:

_____

Section C: Multiplication

Short-answer questions

Specific instructions to students

- This section is designed to help you improve your multiplication skills when working with fractions.
- Read the following questions and answer all of them in the spaces provided.
- You may not use a calculator.
- You need to show all working.

QUESTION 1

Solve $\frac{2}{4} \times \frac{1}{3}$.

Answer:

_____

QUESTION 2

Solve $2\frac{2}{3} \times 1\frac{1}{2}$.

Answer:

_____

QUESTION 3

During the day, an apprentice used two bottles of demineralised water, both of which had been $\frac{2}{3}$ full. What was the total amount of water used?

Answer:

_____

QUESTION 4

A painter uses three tins of 4 L primer that are $\frac{3}{4}$ full. The tins were left over from a previous job. How much primer was used?

Answer:

_____

QUESTION 5

Four small bottles of plumbing pipe weld that are each $\frac{1}{3}$ full are used to connect PVC piping. How much is used in total?

Answer:

Section D: Division

QUESTION 1

Solve $\frac{2}{3}$ divided by $\frac{1}{4}$.

Answer:

QUESTION 2

Solve $2\frac{3}{4}$ divided by $1\frac{1}{3}$.

Answer:

QUESTION 3

An apprentice has four empty containers for paint. She needs to evenly distribute the contents of three larger containers into each of the four so that she can dilute the contents. How much will be in each of the four containers?

Answer:

QUESTION 4

A supervisor has three empty bottles and two full bottles of methylated spirits. He wants to transfer the liquid to the empty bottles evenly. How much of the methylated spirits will be evenly transferred to each of the three empty bottles from the two full bottles?

Answer:

QUESTION 5

A truck driver wants to divide up some hand cleaner into small containers. If there are two bottles of hand cleaner that need to be poured into six empty bottles, how much will be poured into each of the six empty bottles?

Answer:

Shutterstock.com/Dmitry Kalinovsky

Unit 8: Percentages

> **10% rule: Move the decimal one place to the left to get 10%.**

EXAMPLE

10% of $45.00 would be $4.50.

QUESTION 1

A bill for concreter's tools comes to $220.00. The customer gets 10% off.

a What will the discount be?

Answer:

_____

b What will the bill come to after the 10% is taken off?

Answer:

_____

QUESTION 2

A builder buys 10 door gauges for steel doorframes for different house projects. The total cost comes to $225.00. A discount of 10% is given by the store.

a How much will the discount be?

Answer:

_____

b What is the final bill?

Answer:

_____

QUESTION 3

A paver buys pavers that cost $167.50. He receives a discount of 10%.

a How much will the discount be?

Answer:

_____

b What is the final cost?

Answer:

_____

QUESTION 4

A builder purchases a 305 mm compound mitre saw for $359.70. A 5% discount is given.

a How much is the discount worth?

Answer:

_____

b What is the final total? (Hint: Find 10%, halve it and then subtract it from the overall price.)

Answer:

_____

QUESTION 5

A demolition company purchases a high-quality cordless 18 V drill with two batteries with a one-hour charging time for $620, a 240 V 10 A portable four-socket power outlet for $63 and a 600 W belt sander for $120.

a How much is the total?

Answer:

_____

b How much would a 20% discount be?

Answer:

_____

c What is the final cost after discount?

Answer:

_____

QUESTION 6

The following items are purchased for a building
Company by the site manager: a dust-free drywall
sander for $162; a multi-brush cutter 3-in-1 43cc with a
backpack for $187.50; 31cc portable concrete vibrator for
$312; a 220 W chain saw sharpener for $32; and a 1500 W
hammer drill for $56.

a What is the total?

Answer:

_____

b What is would a 10% discount be?

Answer:

_____

c What is the final cost after the discount?

Answer:

_____

QUESTION 7

A hardware store offers '20% off' the price of any
painting and decorating products as long as the
customer spends at least $100. A customer spends $105
on various items in the store. How much would the
customer pay to then also buy a portable tyre inflator air
compressor, with an original price of $39?

Answer:

_____

QUESTION 8

A particular range of painting products are discounted
by 15%. The recommended retail price of low-sheen
paint is $48 for a 4 L tin.

a How much will the discount be?

Answer:

_____

b What is the final price?

Answer:

_____

Shutterstock.com/Nicholas Piccillo

QUESTION 9

A 125 mm drill press vice is priced at $16.90 as the
recommended retail price. The store has a '20% sale'
on this item. What will the sale price be?

Answer:

_____

QUESTION 10

G String line No. 8 × 100 m yellow is priced at $5.90 each.
During a sale the product is sold at '30% off'. What will
the selling price be?

Answer:

_____

Unit 9: Measurement Conversions

QUESTION 1

How many millimeters are in 1 cm?

Answer:

QUESTION 2

How many centimetres are in 1 m?

Answer:

QUESTION 3

How many millimetres are in 1 m?

Answer:

QUESTION 4

If there are two brushstrokes every 2 cm, how many brushstrokes would be in 10 cm?

Answer:

QUESTION 5

How many millilitres are in a 1.5 L bottle of hand cleaner?

Answer:

QUESTION 6

How many metres are in 3500 mm?

Answer:

QUESTION 7

A delivery truck carries materials weighing $\frac{1}{4}$ tonne. How many kilograms is that?

Answer:

QUESTION 8

Delivery trucks deliver 2 tonnes of materials to a building site. How many kilograms is that?

Answer:

QUESTION 9

A semitrailer delivers materials to a worksite that weigh 4750 kg. How many tonnes is that?

Answer:

QUESTION 10

A yard contains demolition material and measures 4.8 m wide and 12 m long. How far is it around the perimeter of the yard?

Answer:

From time to time, it will be important to be able to convert inches and feet into centimetres or metres.

Note: 1 inch equals 2.54 cm or 25.4 mm; 1 foot equals 0.3 m.

QUESTION 11

Brian needed to use a 12 inch premier drywall plastering flat box. How long would the flat box be in centimetres?

Answer:

QUESTION 12

On Tuesday, Paul hires an 11 foot heavy-duty drywall lifter to complete some renovation work at a house. How many metres is 11 feet?

Answer:

QUESTION 13

Jo uses a $\frac{3}{4}$ inch socket on a nut to release it. What size is the socket in millimetres?

Shutterstock.com/mrHanson

Answer:

QUESTION 14

Kev has bought a new 16 foot drywall plasterboard gyprock panel lifter. How many metres is this?

Answer:

QUESTION 15

Pete used a coach bolt that is $3\frac{1}{2}$ inches long to secure part of a frame. How long is $3\frac{1}{2}$ inches in millimetres?

Answer:

QUESTION 16

Michael bought a three-piece 1 inch drywall screw preset driver bits. How long would each piece be millimetres?

Answer:

QUESTION 17

A plasterer uses a 4 inch drywall finishing corner tool on a bedroom. How long is the tool in centimetres and millimetres?

Answer:

QUESTION 18

Jenny is renovating her house and she wants to use plasterboard measuring 3000 mm × 1200 mm. What are these dimensions in metres?

Answer:

QUESTION 19

Chris purchases a 10 inch straight stud and track crimper for metal studs. How long is the tool in centimetres?

Answer:

QUESTION 20

Dana uses 13 mm × 42 mm metal gyprock screws on plasterboard. What are the dimensions of the screws in centimetres?

Answer:

Unit 10: Earning Wages/Work Time

Short-answer questions

Specific instructions to students

- This unit will help you calculate how much a job is worth and how long you need to complete that job.
- Read the following questions and answer all of them in the spaces provided.
- You may not use a calculator.
- You need to show all working.

QUESTION 1

Henry earns $360.60 net (take home) per week as a first-year apprentice. How much does Henry earn per year if this is his regular weekly salary? (Remember: There are 52 weeks in a year.)

Answer:

_____

QUESTION 2

Rocky starts work at a construction site at 8.00 a.m. because of wet weather. He has a break at 10.30 a.m. for 20 minutes. Lunch starts at 12.30 p.m. and finishes at 1.30 p.m. Rocky then works through to 4 p.m.

a How long are the breaks in total?

Answer:

_____

b How many hours have been worked in total, excluding breaks?

Answer:

_____

QUESTION 3

Zach works a 38-hour week at a hardware store and earns $12.50 an hour. How much is his gross earnings (before tax)?

Answer:

_____

QUESTION 4

Melissa gets paid $411 net for her week's work at a major hardware store. She then spends money on the following: a new dress for $36.95, jewellery for $19.55,

$95 on entertainment, CDs worth $59.97 and work socks that cost $12.60 for three pairs.

a What is the total of all money spent?

Answer:

_____

b How much is left?

Answer:

_____

QUESTION 5

Several customers come to a hardware store for a DIY workshop on furnisher construction on a Thursday night. The store assistant takes the following amount of time helping each customer with their DIY projects: 34 minutes, 18 minutes, 7 minutes, 44 minutes and 59 minutes. How much time in total, in minutes and hours, has been taken assisting these customers?

Alamy / © Duane Branch

Answer:

_____

QUESTION 6

A plasterer takes $1\frac{1}{4}$ hours to finish off the cornices in a house.

a   How many minutes is this?

Answer:

_____

b   How many hours are left if the plasterer normally works an eight-hour day?

Answer:

_____

QUESTION 7

During a shift, construction workers complete the following jobs.

- Unload materials from a truck, sort them and use a forklift to distribute the materials to different locations on-site. This takes $1\frac{1}{2}$ hours to complete.

- Check building plans and measure and mark the location of structures. Then haul and hoist materials into place. This takes $1\frac{1}{4}$ hours.

a   How much time, in hours and part hours, has been spent on the two jobs?

Answer:

_____

b   If the construction workers work an eight-hour day, how many hours are left to work in the day, including breaks?

Answer:

_____

QUESTION 8

An equipment hire company charges $125 for hiring a belt sander for a day. The sanding takes 1 hour and 50 minutes to complete.

a   How long will be left in their eight-hour working day for more sanding at a different location? (Give your answer in hours and minutes.)

Answer:

_____

b   How many minutes will the sanding take?

Answer:

_____

QUESTION 9

A site manager begins work at 7 a.m. and works until 4 p.m. He has a morning break of 20 minutes, a lunch break of 60 minutes and an afternoon break of 20 minutes.

a   How much time has been spent on breaks?

Answer:

_____

b   How much time has been spent working?

Answer:

_____

QUESTION 10

An equipment hire company's daily takings come to $1850.50. The manager spent 10 hours at the office working by himself. How much are the hourly takings, on average, per hour?

Answer:

_____

QUESTION 11

An apprentice construction worker works a 38-hour week and has a pay rate of $12.75 per hour. How much is the gross pay before tax?

Answer:

_____

QUESTION 12

A demolition worker works 8 hours each day over a five-day week and then works 5 hours on Saturday morning. The hourly rate that the demolition company pays during the week is $28.50. On weekends they pay $35.75 per hour. What are the gross earnings of the worker for this week?

Answer:

_____

9780170464505

QUESTION 13

A plasterer works a 38-hour week over five days and charges an hourly rate of $30. On Saturday and Sunday, work needs to be completed on a house that is being sold in the next few weeks. The plasterer works 6 hours on both days of the weekend and charges $45 per hour for both days. How much does he earn (gross) for the seven-day week?

Answer:

_____

QUESTION 14

A construction supervisor earns $45.50 per hour and works a 38-hour week. What are her gross wages?

Answer:

_____

QUESTION 15

A welder takes 26 minutes to weld a support to a truss. If 32 supports need welding and each takes a total of 26 minutes to weld, how long will it take to complete all of the welds? (Give your answer in hours and minutes.)

Answer:

_____

Unit 11: Squaring Numbers

Section A: Introducing square numbers

Short-answer questions

Specific instructions to students

- This section is designed to help you both improve your skills and increase your speed in squaring numbers.
- Read the following questions and answer all of them in the spaces provided.
- You may not use a calculator.
- You need to show all working.

Any number squared is multiplied by itself.

EXAMPLE

4 squared $= 4^2 = 4 \times 4 = 16$

QUESTION 1

6 squared =

Answer:

_____

QUESTION 2

8 squared =

Answer:

_____

QUESTION 3

$12^2 =$

Answer:

_____

QUESTION 4

$3^2 =$

Answer:

_____

QUESTION 5

$7^2 =$

Answer:

_____

QUESTION 6

$11^2 =$

Answer:

_____

QUESTION 7

$10^2 =$

Answer:

_____

QUESTION 8

$9^2 =$

Answer:

_____

QUESTION 9

$2^2 =$

Answer:

_____

QUESTION 10

$13^2 =$

Answer:

_____

Section B: Applying square numbers to the trade

QUESTION 1

A 5 m × 5 m area on a set of building plans needs to be graded and levelled. What size is the area in square metres?

Shutterstock.com/Richard Thornton

Answer:

QUESTION 2

A playground measuring 6 m × 6 m needs to be levelled. What is the total size of the area in square metres?

Answer:

QUESTION 3

A building plan has an area on it that shows the floor of a storeroom measuring 12 m × 12 m. This floor needs to be concreted. How many square metres of floor are there?

Answer:

QUESTION 4

A concreter has to smooth and finish poured concrete for a gymnasium floor that measures 15 m × 15 m. How much floor area is this in square metres?

Answer:

QUESTION 5

A demolition crew needs to clear out an area of a backyard that measures 8 m × 8 m. How many square metres is the backyard?

Answer:

QUESTION 6

A construction worker unpacks two boxes of materials for a worksite. The first box contains 4 × 4 bottles of sunscreen. The second box contains 3 × 3 tubes of liquid nails. How many stock items are there in the two boxes in total?

Answer:

QUESTION 7

A pallet of ceramic pots arrives at a hardware store. If they are packed in a 20 × 20 formation, how many are there?

Answer:

QUESTION 8

The following are delivered by truck to a major worksite: a box with 5 × 5 fluted rubbing bricks with handle, 3 × 3 plastering water splash brush emulsion face tools (6 inch), and 10 × 10 tubes of waterproof silicone. How many items of stock are there in total?

Answer:

QUESTION 9

A major equipment hire company has the following equipment stored and aligned in its yard: 5 × 5 scissor lifts, 5 × 5 forklifts and 5 × 5 material handling lifts. How many lifts are there in total?

iStockphoto/mladn61

Answer:

QUESTION 10

A toolkit consists of some of the following items of varying sizes: 3 × 3 drill bits; 2 × 2 insulated screwdrivers; 2 × 2 crimping tools; and 3 × 3 spanners. How many items are there in total?

Answer:

9780170464505

Unit 12: Area and Perimeter

Short-answer questions

Specific instructions to students

- This section is designed to help improve your skills in calculating and simplifying ratios.
- Read the following questions and answer all of them in the spaces provided.
- You may not use a calculator.
- You need to show all working.

QUESTION 1

A worker reads off a building plan that the floor area for a two-storey office building is $23\,m \times 28\,m$. What is the total area and perimeter of the floor?

Answer:

QUESTION 2

On a building plan, an office measures $3\,m \times 4\,m$ and another floor measures $6\,m \times 7\,m$.

a   What is the area of each?

Answer:

b   What is the perimeter of each?

Answer:

c   What is the total area when added together?

Answer:

d   What is the total perimeter when added together?

Answer:

QUESTION 3

A building plan shows that a bathroom area measures $2.2\,m \times 1.8\,m$ and that an office floor measures $4.4\,m \times 5.2\,m$.

a   What is the area of each?

Answer:

b   What is the perimeter of each?

Answer:

QUESTION 4

A fence needs to be erected around the perimeter of a block of land. The lengths of the sides of the block of land are $34.5\,m$. The length of the back of the block is $19.3\,m$. What is the total amount of metres of fencing needed?

Answer:

QUESTION 5

Trenches measuring $600\,mm \times 600\,mm$ need to be dug for sewerage and water on a block of land. The length of each trench varies and each measures $4.3\,m$, $6.9\,m$, $2.1\,m$, $4.7\,m$ and $5.3\,m$. What is the total length of all of the trenches?

Answer:

Unit 13: Ratios

QUESTION 1

A concreter wants to mix a high-strength concrete for part of a building slab. The ratio that is used is 1:2:3 (cement:sand:stone or gravel). If 18 kg is needed to begin with, how many kilograms of each part are required?

Answer:

QUESTION 2

A concreter mixes concrete for finishing off house foundations. The ratio used is 1:3:5 (cement:sand:stone or gravel). If 90 kg is needed to finish off, how many kilograms of each are required for the mix?

Answer:

QUESTION 3

Mortar needs to be mixed for use on a building site. The ratio used is 1:6:1 (general purpose cement:sand:stone or gravel). If a total of 16 kg is estimated to be needed to begin with, how many kilograms of each part are required?

Answer:

QUESTION 4

A landscaper needs to mix fuel for his chainsaw so that he can trim several large trees. The ratio needed is 1:50 (oil to petrol). How much two-stroke oil needs to be added to 5 L of petrol to achieve the correct mix?

Answer:

QUESTION 5

A demolition crew needs to clear a block of land for housing. This includes cutting down several trees using a chainsaw. The mix needed for fuel is 1:50. How much two-stroke oil will need to be added to a 20 L jerry can of petrol to give the correct ratio for the fuel for the chainsaw?

Answer:

Unit 14: Applying Maths to the General Construction Trade

Section A: Digging trenches

QUESTION 1

A trench measures $15\,m \times 600\,mm \times 600\,mm$. If it takes 15 minutes to dig 1 m of the trench to the required dimensions with a trench digger, how long will it take to dig the whole trench?

Answer:

QUESTION 2

A series of trenches measures $12\,m \times 600\,mm \times 600\,mm$ in total. The machinery has broken down and the trenches need to be dug by shovel by two workers. If it takes 35 minutes to dig 1 m of the trenches to the required dimensions by hand, how long will it take to dig the whole trench?

Answer:

QUESTION 3

A trench digger is hired for a week to dig trenches for a house. The cost of hiring the trench digger is $77 per day. If it takes 8 hours a day over a five-day week to complete most of the work, what will the hiring cost be?

Answer:

QUESTION 4

A building and construction company has four jobs on the go. They need a trench digger for work on each site at different times over four months. The equipment is hired at a cost of $308 per week, plus 10% GST. What will the hiring cost be?

Answer:

QUESTION 5

Two trench diggers are hired to dig the trenches for a retirement village. The cost of hiring each trench digger is $77 per day. The construction company hires the equipment for six days over a two-week period. What will the hiring cost be?

Answer:

Section B: Concreting

QUESTION 1

An area measuring $5\,m \times 4\,m \times 15\,cm$ needs to be concreted. How many cubic metres need to be ordered?

Answer:

QUESTION 2

The bedroom floor of an apartment measures $3.8\,m \times 3.2\,m$. The depth of concrete needed is $15\,cm$. What volume of concrete is needed?

Answer:

QUESTION 3

A house has two bedrooms that measure $3.5\,m \times 4.2\,m$ and $4.3\,m \times 3.9\,m$. Concrete needs to be replaced in each room. If the depth of the concrete needs to be $15\,cm$, how many cubic metres of concrete are needed?

Answer:

QUESTION 4

The plan of a three-bedroom house shows four rooms that measure the following: bedroom 1 − $3.3\,m \times 3.6\,m$; bedroom 2 − $2.7\,m \times 3.45\,m$; bedroom 3 − $2.7\,m \times 3.1\,m$; and the family room − $4.3\,m \times 4.0\,m$. Each needs concreting to a depth of $0.15\,m$. What is the total volume?

Answer:

QUESTION 5

The floor plan of a house consists of two rectangular areas: $7.5\,m \times 14.6\,m$ and $3.2\,m \times 7.5\,m$. Concrete needs to be poured in this area to a depth of $0.15\,m$. How many cubic metres of concrete need to be ordered for this part of the building?

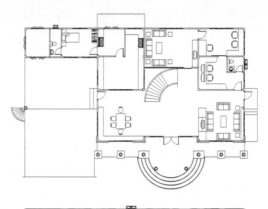

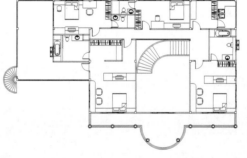

Shutterstock.com/501room

Answer:

Section C: Demolition

Short-answer questions

Specific instructions to students

- This section is designed to help you improve your maths skills in the general construction trade.
- Read the following questions and answer all of them in the spaces provided.
- You may not use a calculator.
- You need to show all working.

Working in demolition can be a challenging job – it is also potentially dangerous. Any given task can cost between $25 and $95 per hour, depending on the task's size and complexity. With an average cost of $61.22 per hour, the hiring of a demolition expert might be something that needs to be considered. There are some hazards associated with demolition that can be dangerous. Demolition is often considered to be high-risk work as there is a possibility that things may go wrong. Examples of problems can include the instability of a structure; poor or excessive loading on the floor; glass damage and, often, fragmentation; adverse weather conditions, including heat and cold; site access, which may be difficult; and the presence of asbestos.

QUESTION 1

A demolition company quotes for the demolition of a small house on a small block of land with easy access. They quote $75 per hour to demolish but not to clear the block. The company says that it will take three weeks to complete, and each week will be a 38-hour working week. How much is the quote from the company?

Answer:

QUESTION 2

Three quotes for the demolition of a house on a block that is 18 m × 33 m with easy access are received by the owners. The first quote is for $65 per hour to demolish. The second quote is for $77 per hour. The third quote is for $84 per hour. All three companies agree that it will take two weeks to complete the demolition, and each week will be a 38-hour working week. How much would each of the quotes be?

Answer:

iStockphoto/Lya_Cattel

QUESTION 3

A demolition company is contracted to demolish a two-storey house. They charge $68 per hour. If the job takes two weeks to complete with two workers on site each day for 38-hour working weeks, how much will the company charge?

Answer:

QUESTION 4

A family receives a quote from a demolition company to demolish and remove all of the debris from their block. The demolition company charges $62 per hour and says it will take eight working days at 8 hours a day to complete the demolition. In addition, the demolition company charges $3500 to remove all the debris, clear the block, grade and level after the demolition. How much did the company charge in total?

Answer:

Section D: Scaffolding

Short-answer questions

Specific instructions to students

- This section is designed to help you improve your maths skills in the general construction trade.
- Read the following questions and answer all of them in the spaces provided.
- You may not use a calculator.
- You need to show all working.

QUESTION 1

A builder requires scaffolding to continue rendering work on the exterior of a house. Rather than hire, the company decides to purchase a 2.5 m × 0.7 m × 5.0 m mobile aluminium scaffold for $3699.00. If 10% GST needs to be added to the price, plus a shipping cost of $250.00, what will the final cost be?

Answer:

QUESTION 2

A construction company purchases a two-level tower with 5.7 m reach height with a guardrail set for $2599.00, plus 10% GST and $475 shipping cost. What is the final total cost of the scaffold equipment?

Shutterstock.com / Vereshchagin Dmitry

Answer:

QUESTION 3

A 3 m deck of scaffolding needs to be hired on a worksite for a number of different jobs for seven days. The best quote the company gets is as follows: $49 per deck height metre per seven-day week, including GST. The cartage rate each way and per unit is $61.50, including GST. What is the total hiring cost?

Answer:

QUESTION 4

A 5 m deck of scaffolding needs to be hired on a worksite for a number of different jobs for a month. The quote the company gets is as follows: $49 per deck height metre per seven-day week, including GST. The cartage rate each way and per unit is $61.50, including GST. The scaffold must be erected by a suitably qualified person. What is the total hiring cost?

Answer:

QUESTION 5

Four 4 m decks of scaffolding are hired for a worksite for three months. The quote the company gets that it considers to be the fairest is: $43 per deck height metre per seven-day week, including GST. The cartage rate each way and per unit is $54.50, including GST. What is the total cost of hiring all four decks for the three months?

Answer:

9780170464505

Section E: Bobcats and heavy machinery

QUESTION 1

A quote for removing debris from renovations and levelling work around a house includes hiring a 1.3 tonne s70 bobcat with a 1180 mm bucket for three days. The quote is for $238 per day. How much will it cost to hire the bobcat for the three days?

Answer:

QUESTION 2

The hire rate for an s70 bobcat is $264 per day. The bobcat is hired out; however, it is returned late and incurs a late fee of $50. In addition, the bobcat needs 4 L of diesel to re-fuel it, costing $1.65 per litre. It was also returned caked with heavy clay and mud and so requires cleaning, incurring a cost of $35. What is the total cost to the hirer?

Answer:

QUESTION 3

A 2.6 tonne 51 hp bobcat, with a 4-in-1 bucket and a lifting capacity of 635 kg, is hired to remove rubbish and soil from a construction site over five days. The daily hire cost is $255.75. How much does it cost for the five-day hire? The job is incomplete at the end of the five days, so the hirer hires the bobcat for one more day at a fee of $311.00. What is the total cost for the six days?

Shutterstock.com / Leah-Anne Thompson

Answer:

QUESTION 4

A construction company wants to hire a 19 foot scissor lift to paint a new building and receives a quote of $120 for 24 hours. The company decides to hire the lift for four days. How much will this cost? The job takes much longer than first thought, so the company hires the lift for another three days. What is the total cost?

Answer:

QUESTION 5

A construction company needs to hire four boom lifts so that steel beams can be welded and painted. The electricians also need to use one to complete the wiring in the ceiling and walls of an industrial complex. The company hires three 45 foot (16 m) diesel 4WD knuckle booms at a cost of $1050 per week and a 30 foot (10.6 m) electrical knuckle boom at a cost $945 per week. The job takes two months to complete and the booms are hired for this period. What is the total cost?

Answer:

General Construction
Practice Written Exam for the General Construction Trade

Reading time: 10 minutes

Writing time: 1 hour 30 minutes

Section A: Literacy
Section B: General Mathematics
Section C: Trade Mathematics

QUESTION and ANSWER BOOK

Section	Topic	Number of questions	Marks
A	Literacy	7	23
B	General Mathematics	11	25
C	Trade Mathematics	43	72
		Total 61	Total 120

The sections may be completed in the order of your choice.
NO CALCULATORS are to be used during the exam.

Spelling

Read the passage below and then underline the 20 spelling errors.

10 marks

Erik knew that he was keen on becoming a construction worker from when he was a child. His dad, who had gone to unaversity, told him to follow his intrests and do what he enjoyed doing and make that his career. Erik enjoyed the idea of working with others, and he had assisted tradspeople on building and construction sites during work experience during Year 11of high school. He had spent many hours working with his friend Gerry, doing a range of manuel laboring jobs.

Erik had learned that construction workers parform a range of tasks and on-site he and Gerry had unloaded, carried and stacked building matarials. Their crew also consisted of Greg and Mike who helped to place tools and equipment in position for the tradesmen. All four would dig trenches with hand tools or jackhamers so that they could break up rock and concrete. This would mean that footings and services could be laid. Greg and Mike worked together to erect scafolding and Greg was certified in this area. Mike was good at mixing, pouring and spreading concrete, and he could easily use wheelbarows to remove debris from building sites.

Erik and Gerry decided that they could expand their job oportunities if they undertook on-site or short-course traning. They agreed, with Greg and Mike, that they might consider jobs like concrate workers, doggers, riggers and scaffolders or steel fixers if they could get more qualificetions in these areas.

Lynda is the construction project manager who is responcible for cordinating the construction of large building projects that Erik, Gerry, Greg and Mike worked on. She gave the crew some great ideas about working on a range of projects that could include hotels, factories, office blocks, home unit devlopments, schools, hospitals and large housing developments. Lynda sugested that this would enhance each worker's experience and assist them in understanding the skills needed to complete the projects. She mentioned that they should also consider getting experience in interprating plans and working on suparvising people working on a range of projects, and learn how to negotiate with building owners and subcontractors.

Correct the spelling errors by writing them out with the correct spelling below.

Answer:

_____

_____

_____

Alphabetising

Put the following words into alphabetical order.

7 marks

Hard hat	Chainsaw
Crane	Support
WHS (Work Health and Safety)	Jackhammer
Scissor lift	Extension cord
Materials handling	Overalls
Personal protective equipment	Welder
Bobcat	Hoist

Answer:

_____

_____

_____

_____

_____

_____

_____

_____

_____

_____

_____

_____

_____

_____

_____

_____

_____

Comprehension

Short-answer questions

Specific instructions to students

- Read the passage and then answer the questions that follow using full sentences.

Rocco was keen to become a crane operator as he had read about the construction industry and he had completed work during the holidays with his uncle on-site. He had thought about what he was going to do once he left school and he knew that working was his preferred option rather than going to university. The thought of using cranes to lift, move and place objects interested him, and moving from location to location on construction sites motivated him to finish school. His best friend Stratos was a crane operator already, and he told Rocco about what he did when he first arrived at the worksite. He needed to check the condition of the ground before setting up the crane and, when he needed to, he would place timber blocks or steel plates under the outrigger pads of the crane.

Tony, the site supervisor, would also check that the crane was level on the outriggers before attempting to lift any loads.

Stratos was trained in the many aspects to do with operating his crane, including being aware of how much material can be safely hoisted in each load according to the crane's capacity and respecting the weather conditions. He needed to make sure that his crane was ready by checking all of the controls, instruments and gauges before lifting any loads. Stratos is part of a team and once he had moved the crane and positioned the hook, the diggers could then attach any load, sling, shackle and / or chains.

QUESTION 1   1 mark

Why was Rocco keen to become a construction worker?

Answer:

_____

_____

_____

QUESTION 2   1 mark

What interested Rocco about the construction industry?

Answer:

_____

_____

_____

QUESTION 3   1 mark

What did Stratos need to do when he first arrived at the site to set up his crane?

Answer:

_____

_____

_____

_____

QUESTION 4   2 marks

What are two of the areas that Stratos was trained in with respect to setting his crane up at a worksite?

Answer:

_____

_____

_____

_____

QUESTION 5   1 mark

What needed to be checked on the crane before lifting any loads?

Answer:

_____

_____

Section B: General Mathematics

QUESTION 1   3 marks
What unit of measurement would you use to measure:

a   concrete

Answer:

_____

b   temperature of oil

Answer:

_____

c   amount of oil?

Answer:

_____

QUESTION 2   3 marks
Give examples of how the following might be used in
the concreting industry.

a   Percentage

Answer:

_____

b   Decimal

Answer:

_____

c   Fraction

Answer:

_____

QUESTION 3   2 marks
Convert the following units.

a   1 kg to grams

Answer:

_____

b   1500 g to kilograms

Answer:

_____

QUESTION 4   1 mark
Write the following in descending order.

0.7   0.71   7.1   70.1   701.00   7.0

Answer:

_____

QUESTION 5   2 marks
Write the decimal number that is between:

a   0.1 and 0.2

Answer:

_____

b   1.3 and 1.4.

Answer:

_____

QUESTION 6   2 marks
Round off the following numbers to two (2) decimal
places.

a   5.177

Answer:

_____

b   12.655

Answer:

_____

QUESTION 7   2 marks
Estimate the following by approximation.

a 101×81

Answer:

_____

b 399×21

Answer:

_____

QUESTION 8   2 marks

What do the following add up to?

a $25, $13.50 and $165.50

Answer:

_____

b $4, $5.99 and $229.50

Answer:

_____

QUESTION 9   2 marks

Subtract the following.

a   196 from 813

Answer:

_____

b   5556 from 9223

Answer:

_____

QUESTION 10   2 marks

Use division to solve the following.

a $4824 \div 3$

Answer:

_____

b $84.2 \div 0.4$

Answer:

_____

QUESTION 11   4 marks

Use BODMAS to solve the following.

a $(3 \times 7) \times 4 + 9 - 5$

Answer:

_____

b $(8 \times 12) \times 2 + 8 - 4$

Answer:

_____

Section C: Trade Mathematics

Basic Operations

Addition

QUESTION 1   1 mark

A triangular recreational park is proposed for redevelopment. The area measures 36 m by 44 m by 34 m. What is the total distance around the perimeter of the park?

Answer:

_____

QUESTION 2   1 mark

Three levels cost $15, $14 and $17 respectively. What is the total cost?

Answer:

_____

Subtraction

QUESTION 1   1 mark

A construction worker uses 57 coach bolts from a box that contains 150 coach bolts. How many remain?

Answer:

_____

QUESTION 2   1 mark

An apprentice purchases materials that total $124. The store takes off a discount of $35 during a sale. How much is the total?

Answer:

_____

Multiplication

QUESTION 1   1 mark

A contractor uses six bags of rapid-set cement. If each bag costs $35, what will be the total cost?

Answer:

_____

QUESTION 2   1 mark

Forty-five dust masks are purchased for a worksite. The unit cost of each dust mask is $3. What is the total cost?

Answer:

_____

Division

QUESTION 1   1 mark

A construction company's monthly income is $55 578. What is the company's average weekly income?

Answer:

_____

QUESTION 2   1 mark

At a yearly stocktake, a storeman counts 72 sets of goggles. If 12 goggles are packed into each box, how many boxes are there?

Answer:

_____

Decimals

Addition

QUESTION 1   1 mark

The following building supplies are purchased: centre punch for $8.95, a claw hammer for $13.50 and a welding mask for $24.50. How much do the purchases cost in total?

Answer:

_____

QUESTION 2   1 mark

A trades store sells the following products during an end-of-financial-year sale: brickie's gloves for $7.95, inject mortar for $11.50 and liquid nails for $12.85. How much is the total for all three?

Answer:

_____

Subtraction

QUESTION 1   1 mark

An apprentice earns $418.50 per week. If $35.95 is spent on entertainment and $25.50 is spent on food, how much is left?

Answer:

_____

QUESTION 2   1 mark

A steel support measures 250 cm but needs to be shortened to 224.50 cm. How much of the steel support needs to be cut off?

Answer:

_____

Multiplication

QUESTION 1   2 marks

Three pairs of gloves cost $7.95 each.

a   What is the total cost for all three pairs?

Answer:

_____

b   What change would you get from $50.00?

Answer:

_____

QUESTION 2   2 marks

Four bags of rapid-set cement were purchased for $28.50 each.

a   What was the total cost?

Answer:

_____

b   What change would you get from $120.00?

Answer:

_____

Division

The monthly income for a building company was $208 987. What would be its average weekly income?

Answer:

_____

QUESTION 2   2 marks
A two-hour WHS seminar on first aid costs $196 for seven workers. How much is this per worker?

Answer:

_____

Fractions

QUESTION 1   1 mark
$\frac{1}{4} + \frac{1}{2}$

Answer:

_____

QUESTION 2   1 mark
$\frac{4}{5} - \frac{1}{3}$

Answer:

_____

QUESTION 3   1 mark
$\frac{2}{3} \times \frac{1}{4}$

Answer:

_____

QUESTION 4   1 mark
$\frac{3}{4} \div \frac{1}{2}$

Answer:

_____

Percentages

QUESTION 1   2 marks
A hardware store has a '10% off sale' on all items. If a worker purchases materials totaling $149.00, what is the final sale price?

Answer:

_____

QUESTION 2   2 marks
A plasterer charges a price of $120.00 for squaring up arches. He offers a one-off 20% discount. How much will the customer pay after the discount?

Answer:

_____

Measurement Conversions

QUESTION 1   2 marks
How many grams are in 1.85 kg of tile cement?

Answer:

_____

QUESTION 2   2 marks
How many centimetres do 35 mm convert into?

Answer:

_____

Earning Wages/Work Time

QUESTION 1   2 marks

A construction worker works a 38-hour week and gets paid $14.75 per hour. What is the gross pay for the week?

Answer:

_____

QUESTION 2   2 marks

A laborer works a 38-hour week and then works on a Saturday for five hours. The rate of pay for the 38-hour week is $14 per hour, and the rate of pay for the Saturday is time and a half, which comes to $21 per hour. How much is earned for the six days?

Answer:

_____

Squaring Numbers

QUESTION 1   1 mark

What is 7^2?

Answer:

_____

QUESTION 2   2 marks

The area of a warehouse floor to be concreted measures 13×13 m. What is the total floor area?

Answer:

_____

Area and Perimeter

QUESTION 1   2 marks

A paver needs to clear a block that is 8 m $\times$ 3 m.

a   What is the total area?

Answer:

_____

b   What is the total perimeter?

Answer:

_____

QUESTION 2   2 marks

An area on a set of building plans for the floor of a sports stadium measures 34 m $\times$ 32 m.

a   What is the total area?

Answer:

_____

b   What is the total perimeter?

Answer:

_____

Ratios

QUESTION 1   2 marks

A fuel mix needs to be made up for a chainsaw using the ratio of $1:50$. How much two-stroke oil is needed to add to 5 L of petrol?

Answer:

_____

QUESTION 2   2 marks

Concrete is mixed in the ratio of $1:2:4$. How much of each component is required if a total of 14 kg of cement is needed?

Answer:

_____

Applying Maths to the General Construction Trade

Digging trenches

QUESTION 1   2 marks

A trench 6 m $\times$ 600 mm $\times$ 600 mm needs to be dug for a section of sewerage pipe. If a laborer takes 60 minutes to dig 1 m of the trench, how long will it take to dig the whole trench?

Answer:

_____

QUESTION 2   2 marks

A trench digger is hired to excavate a trench that measures 30 m × 600 mm × 600 mm. If it takes the machine 15 minutes to dig 1 m, how long will it take to dig the whole trench?

Answer:

Concreting

QUESTION 1   2 marks

A driveway needs concreting and the dimensions are 12 m × 3 m × 0.15 m. How many cubic metres of concrete need to be ordered?

Answer:

QUESTION 2   2 marks

An area measuring 32 m × 35 m × 0.15 m needs to be concreted. What volume of concrete is needed?

Answer:

Demolition

QUESTION 1   3 marks

Three demolition companies give the following quotes for the demolition of a house: Company A – $8650, Company B – $7750 and Company C – $9350. To clear the debris and grade the block, each company adds the following to the demolition quotes: Company A – $1200, Company B – $2500 and Company C – its first quote includes clearing and grading the block. Which quote, in total, is the least expensive?

Answer:

QUESTION 2   3 marks

A house is demolished and the company charges $12 500 for the job. The company that completes the job is also known as an eco-demolisher, and they recycle, re-sell and offer remuneration for the following materials: roof tiles removed, palletised and re-sold – $800; ceiling timbers and beams removed and re-sold – $450; bricks removed, cleaned and re-sold – $200; timber and trusses removed and recycled – $200; steel and metal recycled – $155; concrete crushed and recycled – $135; and plants removed, transplanted and

re-sold – $110. How much would the owners pay after the remuneration?

Answer:

Scaffolding

QUESTION 1   2 marks

A painter purchases a scaffold for $2500.00. GST of 10% needs to be added, as well as $250 for shipping. What is the total cost?

Answer:

QUESTION 2   2 marks

A 3 m deck of scaffolding is hired for $49 per deck height metre per week for one week. Cartage costs a total of $185. What is the total cost?

Answer:

Bobcats and heavy machinery

QUESTION 1   2 marks

A bobcat is needed for the removal of debris and clearing a block after the demolition of a house. The hire rate is $238 per day. How much will it cost to hire the bobcat for the four days?

Answer:

QUESTION 2   2 marks

A bobcat is hired for $245 per day to clear, level and grade a block of land. It takes five days to complete the job. What is the cost of hiring the bobcat?

Answer:

QUESTION 3   3 marks

A 2.6 tonne 51 hp bobcat, with a 4-in-1 bucket and a lifting capacity of 635 kg, is hired to remove rubbish and soil from a factory demolition site. It takes six days to complete the job. The daily hire cost is $255.75. How much would it cost for the six-day hire?

Answer:

Glossary

Access   Approach or way in.

Area   The measure of a surface that has defined boundaries, such as land and buildings.

Backfill   To fill the earth, any remaining space after placing concrete, brickwork, timber and pipes.

Bearer   A member of floor framing, spanning piers and supporting joists.

Butterfly   Two skillioned roofs with a box gutter in the middle.

Cavity wall   A hollow wall, generally consisting of two brick walls erected 40–50 mm apart, often joined together with ties of metal.

Contractor   A person who agrees by either a written agreement or contract to supply materials and to complete certain types of work for an agreed sum of money.

Debris   The scattered remains of something broken or destroyed; rubble or wreckage.

Demolition   The tearing down of buildings and other structures.

Eave   The lower part of a roof that overhangs the walls.

Excavation   A hole made by removing earth.

Footing   The construction whereby the weight of the structure is transferred from the base structure to the foundation.

Fulcrum   The point on which a lever rests or is supported.

Gyprock   A wall or ceiling constructed of a prefabricated material, such as plasterboard or panelling.

Hazard   Any source of potential damage, harm or adverse health effects on something or someone under certain conditions at work.

Header   A brick laid with its short end to the face of the wall.

Hip   The sloping apex of a roof that starts at the crown and slopes down to the facia board.

Hoist   Any device or machine used in building for lifting materials.

Levelling instrument   A device consisting of a spirit level attached to a sighting tube, the whole of which is mounted on a tripod and used for levelling a surface to a horizontal plane.

Mitre guide   A device that measures any corner and transfers the correct mitre angle directly to the mitre saw or cutting machine.

Pitch   For rafters, the angle of the rafters taken from the pitching point on the top plate of the wall to the highest point on the underside of the rafter. (The greater the pitch, the faster water flows out of it and the greater chance of gutter failure.)

Plasterboard   A rigid insulating board, usually made of plastering material, often covered both sides with heavy paper.

Retaining wall   Any wall subjected to lateral pressure and built to retain material.

Ridge   The horizontal straight apex of a roof.

Rise   The vertical distance from the top of the top plate to the ridge.

Scaffolding   A temporary structure erected to support access platforms or working platforms.

Skillion   A flat roof that has a visually significant pitch.

Span   The horizontal distance between walls.

Stud   The vertical member in wall framing.

Trowel   A flat-bladed hand tool for levelling, spreading or shaping substances, such as cement.

White card   A nationally agreed competency unit for general induction for construction work.

Wood float   A flat-surfaced tool that is used for smoothing the surface of concrete before it sets.

Work Health and Safety   A cross-disciplinary area that is concerned with protecting the safety, health and welfare of people engaged in any work environment or employment. The main goal of work safety and health programs is the fostering of a safe and healthy work environment for anyone employed or participating in work.

Formulae and Data

Area

Area = length × breadth and is given in square units.

$$= l \times b$$

BODMAS

To solve using BODMAS, in order from left to right, solve the Brackets first, then Of, then Division, then Multiplication, then Addition and lastly Subtraction. The following example has been done for your reference.

EXAMPLE

Solve $(4 \times 7) \times 2 + 6 - 4$.

STEP 1

Solve the Brackets first: $(4 \times 7) = 28$.

STEP 2

No Division, so next solve Multiplication: $28 \times 2 = 56$.

STEP 3

Addition is next: $56 + 6 = 62$.

STEP 4

Subtraction is the last process: $62 - 4 = 58$.

FINAL ANSWER:

58

Volume of a rectangle

Volume = length × width × height and is given in cubic units.

$$= l \times w \times h$$

Times tables

1
1 × 1 = 1
2 × 1 = 2
3 × 1 = 3
4 × 1 = 4
5 × 1 = 5
6 × 1 = 6
7 × 1 = 7
8 × 1 = 8
9 × 1 = 9
10 × 1 = 10
11 × 1 = 11
12 × 1 = 12

2
1 × 2 = 2
2 × 2 = 4
3 × 2 = 6
4 × 2 = 8
5 × 2 = 10
6 × 2 = 12
7 × 2 = 14
8 × 2 = 16
9 × 2 = 18
10 × 2 = 20
11 × 2 = 22
12 × 2 = 24

3
1 × 3 = 3
2 × 3 = 6
3 × 3 = 9
4 × 3 = 12
5 × 3 = 15
6 × 3 = 18
7 × 3 = 21
8 × 3 = 24
9 × 3 = 27
10 × 3 = 30
11 × 3 = 33
12 × 3 = 36

4
1 × 4 = 4
2 × 4 = 8
3 × 4 = 12
4 × 4 = 16
5 × 4 = 20
6 × 4 = 24
7 × 4 = 28
8 × 4 = 32
9 × 4 = 36
10 × 4 = 40
11 × 4 = 44
12 × 4 = 48

5
1 × 5 = 5
2 × 5 = 10
3 × 5 = 15
4 × 5 = 20
5 × 5 = 25
6 × 5 = 30
7 × 5 = 35
8 × 5 = 40
9 × 5 = 45
10 × 5 = 50
11 × 5 = 55
12 × 5 = 60

6
1 × 6 = 6
2 × 6 = 12
3 × 6 = 18
4 × 6 = 24
5 × 6 = 30
6 × 6 = 36
7 × 6 = 42
8 × 6 = 48
9 × 6 = 54
10 × 6 = 60
11 × 6 = 66
12 × 6 = 72

7
1 × 7 = 7
2 × 7 = 14
3 × 7 = 21
4 × 7 = 28
5 × 7 = 35
6 × 7 = 42
7 × 7 = 49
8 × 7 = 56
9 × 7 = 63
10 × 7 = 70
11 × 7 = 77
12 × 7 = 84

8
1 × 8 = 8
2 × 8 = 16
3 × 8 = 24
4 × 8 = 32
5 × 8 = 40
6 × 8 = 48
7 × 8 = 56
8 × 8 = 64
9 × 8 = 72
10 × 8 = 80
11 × 8 = 88
12 × 8 = 96

9
1 × 9 = 9
2 × 9 = 18
3 × 9 = 27
4 × 9 = 36
5 × 9 = 45
6 × 9 = 54
7 × 9 = 63
8 × 9 = 72
9 × 9 = 81
10 × 9 = 90
11 × 9 = 99
12 × 9 = 108

10
1 × 10 = 10
2 × 10 = 20
3 × 10 = 30
4 × 10 = 40
5 × 10 = 50
6 × 10 = 60
7 × 10 = 70
8 × 10 = 80
9 × 10 = 90
10 × 10 = 100
11 × 10 = 110
12 × 10 = 120

11
1 × 11 = 11
2 × 11 = 22
3 × 11 = 33
4 × 11 = 44
5 × 11 = 55
6 × 11 = 66
7 × 11 = 77
8 × 11 = 88
9 × 11 = 99
10 × 11 = 110
11 × 11 = 121
12 × 11 = 132

12
1 × 12 = 12
2 × 12 = 24
3 × 12 = 36
4 × 12 = 48
5 × 12 = 60
6 × 12 = 72
7 × 12 = 84
8 × 12 = 96
9 × 12 = 108
10 × 12 = 120
11 × 12 = 132
12 × 12 = 144

Multiplication grid

×	1	2	3	4	5	6	7	8	9	10	11	12
1	1	2	3	4	5	6	7	8	9	10	11	12
2	2	4	6	8	10	12	14	16	18	20	22	24
3	3	6	9	12	15	18	21	24	27	30	33	36
4	4	8	12	16	20	24	28	32	36	40	44	48
5	5	10	15	20	25	30	35	40	45	50	55	60
6	6	12	18	24	30	36	42	48	54	60	66	72
7	7	14	21	28	35	42	49	56	63	70	77	84
8	8	16	24	32	40	48	56	64	72	80	88	96
9	9	18	27	36	45	54	63	72	81	90	99	108
10	10	20	30	40	50	60	70	80	90	100	110	120
11	11	22	33	44	55	66	77	88	99	110	121	132
12	12	24	36	48	60	72	84	96	108	120	132	144

Notes

Notes